W9-ANP-615

Snap
books

No-Sew
HEADBANDS, BELTS,
AND OTHER ACCESSORIES

by Carly J. Bacon

CAPSTONE PRESS
a capstone imprint

Snap Books are published by Capstone Press,
1710 Roe Crest Drive, North Mankato, Minnesota 56003
www.mycapstone.com

Library of Congress Cataloging-in-Publication Data
Names: Bacon, Carly J., author.
Title: No-sew headbands, belts, and other accessories / by Carly J. Bacon.
Description: North Mankato, Minnesota : Capstone Press, 2019. | Series: Snap
  books. No sew, no problem | Audience: Ages 9-14.
Identifiers: LCCN 2018011001 (print) | LCCN 2018015973 (ebook) |
  ISBN 9781543525601 (eBook PDF) |
  ISBN 9781543525526 (library binding)
Subjects: LCSH: Textile crafts—Juvenile literature. | Dress accessories—Juvenile literature.
Classification: LCC TT699 (ebook) | LCC TT699 .B33 2019 (print) | DDC 646/.3—dc23
LC record available at https://lccn.loc.gov/2018011001

Editorial Credits
Abby Colich, editor; Kayla Rossow, designer; Jo Miller photo researcher;
Laura Manthe, production specialist

Image Credits
All photographs by Capstone Studio: Karon Dubke, Craft Product Producers: All done by
Jodi Roelofs

Design Elements: Capstone and Shutterstock

The author dedicates this book to her parents, Don and Joanne, for their unconditional love
and support.

Printed in the United States of America.
PO1156

Table of Contents

No Sew, All Fun

Who wore it best? When you make your own accessories, the answer will always be you! Creating your own earrings, necklaces, or headbands allows you to add your own unique twist or style to every outfit. Are you worried that you can't sew or don't think you're crafty enough? That's OK! These projects are easy and require no sewing! Fashionable accessories are easy to make. Feel free to experiment or change the steps to make the style your own. Rules are meant to be broken—for both fashion and crafting!

Stick to It

When making accessories, several alternatives to a needle and thread are available. For some projects glue guns or fabric glue work best to fasten things together. When using fabric glue, make sure the label reads "permanent fabric adhesive" or something similar. For other projects, you'll simply tie pieces together or use a connector ring.

Stay Safe

Making your own accessories is fun and easy—as long as you take all necessary safety precautions. Be sure you have an adult to help when using a hot glue gun. A glue gun can become very hot and cause burns if not used with caution. Also make sure an adult is nearby to help when using a craft knife.

⊱⊱⊱⊱⊰ Place Mat Clutch ⊱⊱⊱⊱⊰

You found the perfect dress, but despite all your searching, you can't find a purse to match. Stop searching and make your own. Use an old place mat to create a clutch. Wear it with a shoulder-length strap that shows it off.

What You'll Need

- rectangular place mat
- fabric glue
- clothespins
- measuring tape or ruler
- magnetic snap with prongs
- craft knife

- ribbon
- scissors
- nylon or faux leather strap
- beads, sequins, and other embellishments, if desired

What You'll Do

step 1

step 3

1. Lay the place mat right side down on your work space with the short edges at the top and bottom. Fold the bottom up three-fourths of the way. Add a line of glue around the edges, to glue in place. Wipe up any excess glue with a damp cloth. Use clothespins to hold in place. Let dry completely.

2. Measure to find the center of the top edge. Line up the metal prongs of your magnetic snap and make small marks where the prongs will be inserted. Use a craft knife to cut small slits. Insert the prongs of the snap and secure on the other side.

3. Fold down the top section of the place mat. Make a small mark where the other half of the metal snap will go, lining up the prongs and making a mark for each. Use the craft knife to cut small slits for the prongs. Be careful not to cut through the other end of the purse. Slip the prongs into the holes and secure on the other side.

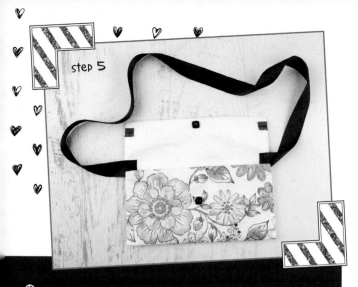

step 5

4. Flip the place mat over. Measure along the top and add 2 inches (5.1 cm). Cut your ribbon to size. Glue the ribbon along the top edge of the place mat. Make sure that the ribbon covers the prongs of the magnetic snap. Secure the extra length of the ribbon on each end of the other side with more glue. Let dry completely.

5. To add a strap, drape the nylon strap over your shoulder. Measure the ends to where you want your purse to hang. Then cut the strap to that length. Glue one end of the strap to the inside of the purse. Repeat on the other side. Add embellishments, if desired.

Tip

A vinyl place mat will be more difficult to fold. Use a woven or fabric place mat for best results. If you don't have an old one at home, check your local thrift store.

Flower Ring

Make a statement with this flower ring! Try making more than one in different colors. You'll have an accessory to match every outfit in your closet.

What You'll Need

- ribbon, 18 inches (45.7 cm)
- ruler
- scissors
- craft wire, 13 inches (33 cm) long
- wire cutter
- fabric glue
- clothespin
- self-adhesive rhinestone jewels

What You'll Do

1. Cut a V shape into the ribbon about 2 inches (5.1 cm) in from one end. Discard the small triangle of fabric.

2. Place the craft wire into the bottom of the V and tie the ribbon in a knot around the wire.

3. Place the wire over your ring finger. Wrap each end of the wire loosely around your finger so that you have a loose-fitting ring. The remaining ends of the wire should point toward the top.

4. Slip the wire off your finger and wrap each end two to three times in a circle around the ribbon knot. Cut off any extra wire with the wire cutter.

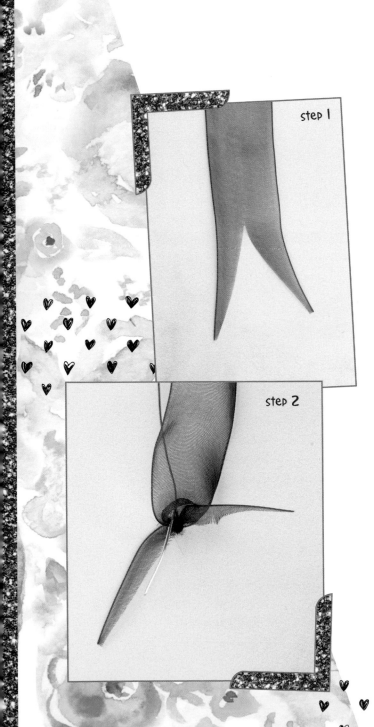

step 1

step 2

5. Take the long end of the ribbon and twist it tightly. Hold the middle down with your thumb so that it remains flat. Continue to twist until you have three to four rows of ribbon, creating a rose shape.

6. Use fabric glue to attach the end of your ribbon to the underside of the ring. Cut off any excess ribbon that sticks out.

7. Place a clothespin on the glued part of your rose. Let dry completely for up to 24 hours.

8. Glue jewels to the center of the rose.

step 5

Braided Belt

Hip slung belts are the perfect answer for adding shape to a loose-fitting shirt or dress. These belts are inexpensive and fast to make. Try creating one to match multiple outfits or make several in different colors.

What You'll Need

- tape measure
- scissors
- suede cord
- silk cord
- 2 connector rings
- hanger

What You'll Do

1. Measure around your waist. Take that measurement, double it, and add 6 inches (15.2 cm). Cut two suede cords and one silk cord to that size.

2. Line up the suede and silk cords so that one end of each are together. Check the other end to make sure all cords are the same length. Trim cords to match if needed.

3. Feed the cord through the connector rings. Fold cords in half with the connector rings at the fold. Tie a knot about 2 inches (5.1 cm) down from the fold, creating a loop for the rings.

4. Secure the loop to a hanger. Hang it somewhere to allow you enough room to braid the cords. Separate the strings into three pairs of two, matching the same materials. Braid the cord pairs until 5 inches (12.7 cm) are left at the end. Tie all six ends in one knot where the braid ends. Tie additional knots at the end of each string.

5. Remove from the hanger. Wrap the belt around your waist. Tie or loop the ends of the belt through the connecter rings.

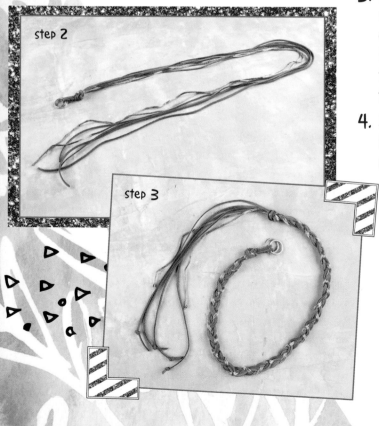

step 2

step 3

More DIY Belts

Braiding cords is a quick and easy way to make belts and other accessories. Try some of these ideas!

✕ Swap the suede and silk for different braidable materials, such as yarn, rope, or ribbon.

✕ Add beads by stringing them onto the cords as you braid.

✕ Try more complicated ways of weaving or knotting.

✕ Try fabric! Measure and cut a length of fabric a little over twice your desired width. Fold the long edges in and hand stitch or glue into place to make a hem.

✕ For a stiffer belt, glue the fabric over thin, bendable cardboard.

✕ Replace the connecter rings with hook and eye clasps or a belt buckle.

Braided Scarf

Whether you live somewhere with freezing temperatures or in a climate with just a few cool days, everyone needs a scarf. Scarves both help keep you warm and make a fashion statement. This braided scarf is the perfect double duty accessory.

What You'll Need

- solid colored piece of fabric, 50 x 18 inches (127 x 45.7 cm)
- scissors
- patterned piece of fabric, 50 x 36 inches (127 x 91.4 cm)
- hair tie
- fabric glue
- coordinating piece of fabric, 12 x 5 inches (30.5 cm x 12.7 cm)

step 3

What You'll Do

1. Fold the solid piece of fabric in half with the long sides touching. Cut the fabric in half along the crease.

2. Gather one end of the short side from the solid and patterned pieces of fabric. Secure together with a hair tie.

3. Braid together the first 12 inches (30.5 cm) of three pieces of fabric. Tie a knot at the end of the braid to secure.

4. Tuck each loose end of fabric into the hair tie to create a circle.

5. Dab some fabric glue where the hair tie connects the fabric. Begin to tightly wrap the small coordinating piece of fabric around this area to conceal it. Dab glue on the other end to secure it in place. Let dry completely.

step 5

Tassel Earrings

Why spend a lot of money on tassel earrings when you can make your own? Not only is this bling inexpensive to make, but you can also make it stand out by adding ribbon.

What You'll Need

- 2 fabric strips, 22 x 0.25 inches (55.9 x 0.6 cm) each
- piece of cardboard, 2 inches (5.1 cm) long
- scissors
- embroidery thread, 4 inches (10.2 cm) long

- 2 pieces of fabric ribbon, each 4 inches (10.2 cm) long
- 2 crimps
- jewelry pliers
- 2 jump rings
- 2 earring hooks

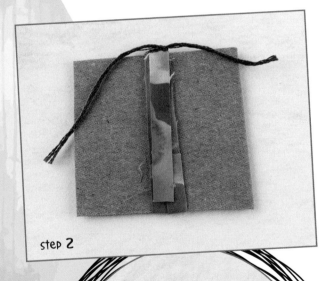

step 2

step 3

What You'll Do

1. Wrap one fabric strip around the cardboard four or five times. Make sure to end at the same spot you began. Cut off any excess.

2. Slip the embroidery thread between the cardboard and the wrapped fabric strip. Tie a knot around the thread pieces opposite to where you began and ended.

3. Slip the fabric off the cardboard. Cut through the loop at the end opposite from where it's tied together with the thread.

4. Line up one edge of the ribbon with the top of the fringe. Slip the top of the fringe and ribbon into the crimp. Press firmly with pliers to close.

5. Use the pliers to open the jump ring. Slip the ring through the hole in the crimp.

6. Slip the jump ring onto the earring hook. Twist the jump ring to close it.

7. Repeat steps 1 through 6 for the other earring.

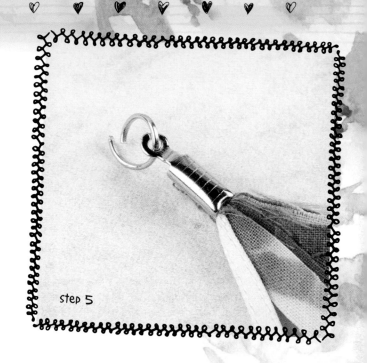

step 5

Fabric Square Earrings

Who knew you could cover cardboard with ribbon to make a pair of glamorous earrings? Add a dangling charm or bead to make these funky or classic, depending on your style.

What You'll Need

- fabric glue
- 4 pieces of fabric, 1 x 1 inch (2.5 x 2.5 cm) each
- 2 cardboard squares, 1 x 1 inch (2.5 x 2.5 cm) each
- scissors
- craft knife
- 4 jump rings
- 2 dangle charms
- 2 lever back ear wires
- embellishments, if desired

What You'll Do

1. Glue one piece of fabric to the front of one cardboard square, covering it evenly. Glue another piece of fabric to the other side of the square. Let dry completely. Use scissors to trim off any frayed edges.

2. Punch a tiny hole in the top center of one edge of your square with a craft knife.

3. Twist open a jump ring and slip on your charm. Slip the open jump ring through the tiny hole you created in the cardboard square. Twist the jump ring closed.

4. Create another tiny hole above your first hole. Insert another jump ring. Slip a lever back ear wire onto your second jump ring. Twist the jump ring closed.

step 3

5. Embellish earrings with your choice of sequins, beads, or glitter, if desired.

6. Repeat steps 1 through 5 for the second earring. Allow both earrings to dry for 24 hours.

Tip

Try cutting a rectangle or different shape from the cardboard.

Flower Hair Clip

Having a bad hair day? Here's one solution to add some flair to your hair. Everyone will be impressed to hear you made it yourself.

What You'll Need

- pencil
- traceable circle, about 1.5 inches (3.8 cm) in diameter
- thin piece of cardboard
- scissors
- dark-colored cotton fabric, about 18 x 21 inches (45.7 x 53.3 cm)
- fabric chalk
- light-colored cotton fabric, about 18 x 21 inches (45.7 x 53.3 cm)
- hot glue gun and glue
- small silver beads
- snap hair clip

step 3

step 7

step 9

What You'll Do

1. Trace a circle onto the cardboard and cut out.

2. Trace four circles onto the dark fabric using fabric chalk and cut out. Trace three circles onto the light fabric and cut out.

3. Take one dark fabric circle and fold in half. Then fold in half again. Secure the inside of the second fold with a small dab of hot glue.

4. Repeat step 3 with the remaining fabric circles.

5. Put a small line of hot glue down one half of the cardboard circle. Place one dark-colored circle on the glue. Make sure the rounded edge of the fabric is lined up with the rounded edge of the cardboard. The cardboard should not be sticking out or showing outside the edge of the fabric.

6. Repeat step 6 with the remaining dark circles. Make sure that fabric pieces evenly cover the cardboard like a pie.

7. Put a line of hot glue down the center of one of the light pieces of folded fabric. Place on top of the dark fabric. Repeat with the remaining two pieces of light fabric, evenly spacing them apart so that an equal amount of dark fabric shows between each.

8. Put a couple of drops of glue in the center where the tips of the folded fabric meet. Gently place your beads on top. Let dry completely.

9. Now glue your cardboard onto the thicker end of your snap clip.

A Bouquet of Hair Clips

Want to make more flower hair clips with different flowers? It's easy! Try these methods:

✗ Take a strip of fabric and fold in half lengthwise. Cut slits about halfway through both layers of the open ends, about every 0.5 inch (1.3 cm). Roll up starting at one end, adding dabs of glue to secure. Fluff open the cut ends after gluing the bottom to your base.

✗ Take a strip of fabric and glue one end to your base. Twist and wrap around the starting point, gluing to the base you as go.

✗ Trace a circle about 4 inches (10.2 cm) wide onto the backside of pattern fabric and cut out. Make a small circle in the center of the backside of the fabric. Take one edge and glue to the center circle. Repeat for the opposite edge and then the other sides so that you've glued in four "corners" of the circle. You should have a square. Glue all four corners of the square to the center. Add a bead or charm to the center.

Natural Dye Headband

Sometimes you just need to keep your hair out of your face. Why not dye some fabric to create a headband like no other? Try making more than one to give to your friends so you can match!

What You'll Need

- 1 cup beet skins
- 6 cups (1.4 L) water
- large cooking pots
- strainer
- bowl
- 1 cup (240 mL) vinegar

- 2 strips of white jersey cotton fabric, 2 x 25 inches (5.1 x 63.5 cm) each
- tongs
- fabric glue
- scissors

What You'll Do

1. Place the beet skins and 2 cups (480 mL) of water in a large pot. Let simmer on medium heat for 1 hour.

2. Remove the pot from the burner. Allow to cool until it is at room temperature.

3. Strain out any pieces of beet skin. Transfer the dyed water to a bowl.

4. Add vinegar, 4 cups (960 mL) of water, and one strip of fabric to a clean pot. Simmer on medium for 1 hour. Remove pot from heat.

5. Use tongs to carefully remove the fabric from the pot. Rinse the fabric in cold water. Wring out any excess water. Place the wet fabric into your bowl of beet water and allow it to soak until it reaches your desired color. The longer you let it soak, the darker it will be.

6. Wring out your fabric. Hang it somewhere until it is completely dry. Make sure it doesn't drip on anything that can be stained. You can also lay it on an old towel.

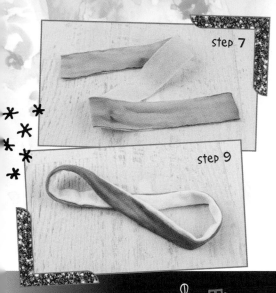

step 7

step 9

7. Take the other piece of fabric and lay both pieces out on your work space right side to right side. Use a thin line of fabric glue to attach both long edges together, creating a tube. Let dry completely.

8. Pull the fabric tube right side out so you are looking at the right side of the fabrics. Wrap the fabric around your head twice to check the length. Cut off any excess fabric.

9. Use fabric glue to attach the ends of your fabric, creating one large circle. Let dry completely.

Tip

You can use other plants such as berries, onion skins, and cabbage for natural dyes. Have an adult help you research instructions for other natural dyes to create more colors of headbands.

Beaded Headband

Looking for a hairpiece that's a little fancier?
In this headband, a metallic chain is balanced
with colored seed beads. Twist them together to
create a piece to pair with an updo, braid, or bun.

What You'll Need

- tape measure
- ball or craft chain
- jewelry pliers
- scissors
- craft cord
- seed beads
- hair elastic

What You'll Do

1. Measure the length of a headband you already own or the circumference of your head. The tape measure should fall 1 inch (2.5 cm) behind your ears.

2. Adjust the size of the chain to the length of your measurement from step 1 by opening one of the links using the jewelry pliers.

3. Cut your craft cord 4 inches (10.2 cm) longer than the measurement from step 1.

4. String the seed beads on your craft cord, leaving 2 inches (5.1 cm) of space at each end. Tie a knot in the cord at each end to keep the beads in place. Wrap the chain around the beads, twisting together. Tie the ends of the cord around the ends of the chain to secure.

5. Tie one end of the twisted piece to the hair elastic. Tie the other end to the opposite side of the hair elastic. Cut off any extra.

6. Wrap around your head to test the length one more time. Cut off any extra length if needed. Secure the other end to the opposite side of the hair elastic.

step 6

Tip

For a softer look that is still fancy, twist together metallic strips of fabric. Add in the ball chain and leave out the beads or vice versa.

Bracelet Key Chain

Whether it's for your front door, your bike lock, or something else, most people have at least one key to keep track of. Make a bracelet that also serves as a key ring for when you're on the go. Add beads with letters to spell out what the key is for. Make one for all your extra keys and you'll never get them mixed up.

What You'll Need

- decorative elastic
- scissors
- crimp
- jewelry pliers
- jump ring
- lobster clasp
- craft cord, 6 inches (15.2 cm)
- alphabet beads

What You'll Do

1. Wrap elastic around your wrist to measure for size. Cut to desired length, leaving about 0.5 inch (1.3 cm) of extra material.

2. Make sure edges of elastic are cut straight and even. Fold in half. Slip ends inside crimp. Use jewelry pliers to squeeze closed. You may need to fold over the ends a bit before slipping it into the clasp for a better grip.

3. Twist open your jump ring and slip it through the hole in the crimp and through the hole in the lobster clasp. Twist the jump ring closed.

4. Fold craft cord in half and secure around the jump ring by pulling the ends through the fold to create a loop around it.

5. Add alphabet beads to spell out your name or what the key is for. Tie a knot at the bottom to secure the beads in place.

6. Open the clasp and attach your key.

step 3

Circle Key Chain

Instead of a bracelet, make a key chain with leftover scraps of fabric. Trace two circles onto patterned fabric and cut out. Cut out another piece of fabric about 0.5 x 1 inch (1.3 x 2.5 cm). Fold a key ring into the fabric and use fabric glue to attach the inside of one fabric circle. Then glue the backside of the two fabric circles together. Trim off any frayed edges. Attach an iron-on letter with your initial or the initial of someone else you want to give it to as a gift. Make sure an adult helps you with the iron.

Soda Tab Bracelet

Soda tabs are great to reuse in craft projects. If you can't collect any from used soda cans, you can buy them from a craft store. Use some to make a one-of-a-kind bracelet that reflects your one-of-a-kind style.

What You'll Need

- suede cord
- scissors
- 10 to 20 soda tabs
- 5 to 10 circle charms

What You'll Do

1. Wrap the suede cord once around your wrist. Add 10 inches (25.4 cm) and cut. Cut a second suede cord the same length. Tie a knot to connect the two cords together. Leave a 1.5- to 2-inch (3.8- to 5-cm)-long tail.

2. Set a soda tab face-up on your work surface. The small hole should be at the top. Thread one cord through the small hole. The cords' knot should sit inside the hole.

3. Thread the other cord through the soda tab's large hole. Now both cords should be underneath the soda tab.

4. Set a second soda tab on your work surface. It should be positioned the same way as in step 2.

5. Thread the cords through the bottom hole of the second soda tab. Pull the tab up the cords until the top hole of the second tab rests below the bottom hole of the first tab.

6. Pull the left cord up and thread it through the overlapping holes. This cord should go to the left of the cords underneath the tabs.

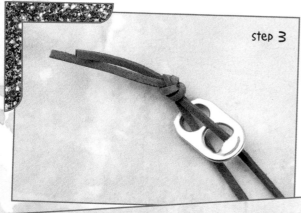

step 3

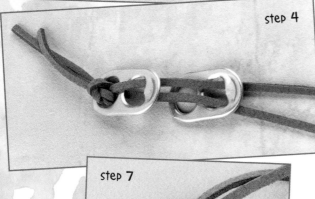

step 4

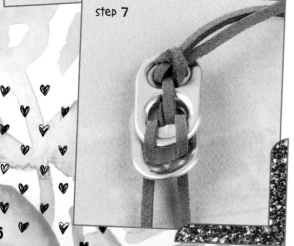

step 7

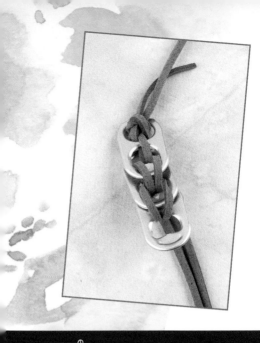

7. Repeat step 6 but with the right cord. The right cord should go to the right of the cords underneath the tabs.

8. Repeat steps 4 through 7.

9. To add some jingle, thread a charm onto a cord after step 5.

10. Repeat steps 4 through 7, adding a charm after every two to three soda tabs.

11. When your bracelet is to your desired length, slip one cord end through the last soda tab's hole. Then tie a knot. Tie the cord ends to the tail you left in step 1. Cut off any excess.

Tip

Have more soda tabs? Use the steps above to make a belt. Fasten it with a connector ring.

Wrap Bracelet

Fashion rules are meant to be broken. You can break all the rules when you make this boho-inspired wrap bracelet. Embellish it with beads that meet your fashion demands. Choose colors to match your best outfit.

What You'll Need

- scissors
- organdy ribbon, 0.25 inch (0.6 cm) wide
- connector bead
- large hole metal beads
- ribbon crimp
- jewelry pliers
- jump ring
- connector ring

What You'll Do

1. Cut one piece of ribbon 42 inches (106.7 cm) long and anothor 22 inches (55.9 cm) long.

2. Fold one ribbon piece in half, lining up the ends evenly. Then slip the folded end through the ring on the connector bead, creating a small loop. Pull the ends of the ribbon through the loop, pulling tightly to secure the ribbon to the connector bead.

3. Repeat step 2 with the other ribbon on the other side of the connector bead.

4. Place the connector bead on the top of your wrist. Wrap the longer pieces of ribbon once around your wrist. Note where the ribbon lands just past the midpoint of your wrist and tie a knot.

5. Beginning at the knot, string a few beads onto the ribbon. Tie another knot to secure beads in place.

6. Place the connector bead on top of your wrist again, this time looping the shorter ribbon around your wrist one and a half times. Note where the end falls in the center of the underside of your wrist. Cut off any extra ribbon, making sure the two ends of the folded ribbon stay even. Slip the two ends into your crimp. Press the crimp together with pliers, securing your ribbon. If the organdy is too thin for the crimp, fold the ribbons over before slipping it in.

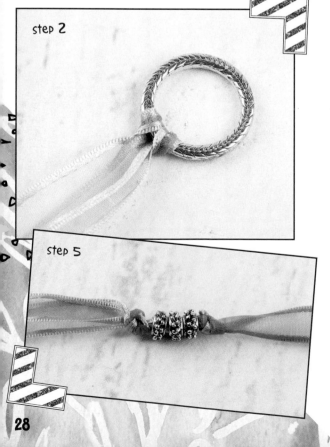

step 2

step 5

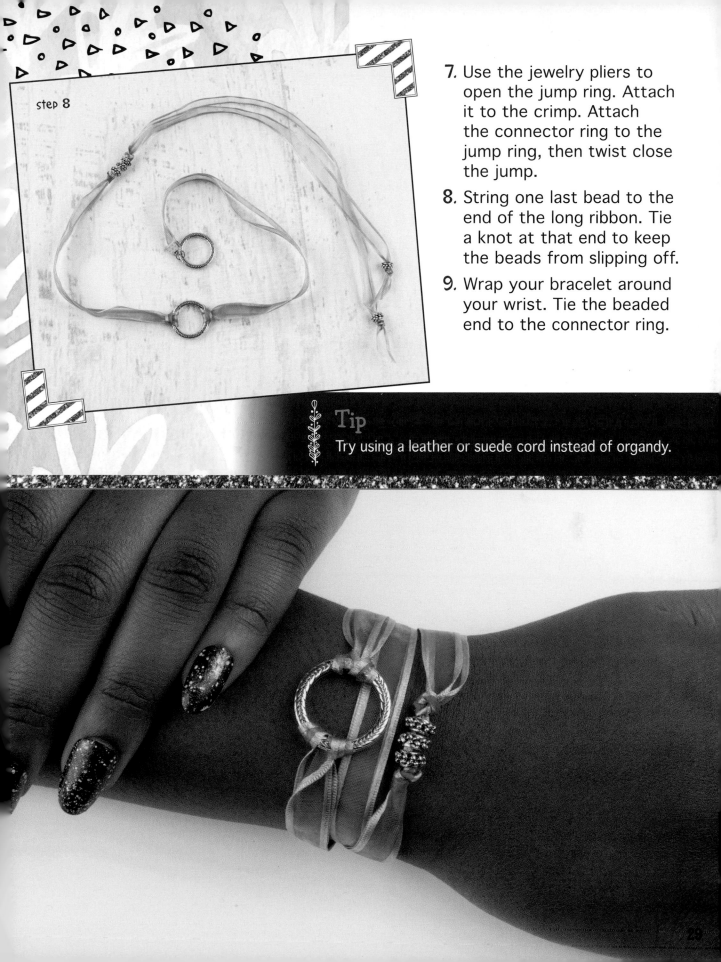

step 8

7. Use the jewelry pliers to open the jump ring. Attach it to the crimp. Attach the connector ring to the jump ring, then twist close the jump.

8. String one last bead to the end of the long ribbon. Tie a knot at that end to keep the beads from slipping off.

9. Wrap your bracelet around your wrist. Tie the beaded end to the connector ring.

Tip

Try using a leather or suede cord instead of organdy.

Fabric Bauble Necklace

This necklace made from fabric won't go unnoticed.
Try painting the wooden beads a color that will
complement your fabric choice.

What You'll Need

- thin, patterned fabric, 30 inches (76.2 cm) long
- 8 wooden craft spheres
- scissors
- 9 large hole beads
- fabric glue
- 2 crimps
- jewelry pliers
- 2 jump rings
- lobster clasp

What You'll Do

1. Wrap the fabric around a craft sphere. Cut the fabric so that it's wide enough to wrap around the sphere two times.

2. Slip fabric into one of the large hole beads. Slide it to the center of the fabric so you have equal lengths of fabric on each side. If the bead is loose and will slide around, remove and tie a knot in the middle of the fabric for the bead to rest on.

3. Insert a craft sphere into the fabric next to the large hole bead. Wrap the sphere completely inside the fabric. Dab with a bit of fabric glue to hold in place. Repeat with another craft sphere on the other side of the large hole bead.

4. Place another large hole bead on one side, sliding the fabric through until it reaches the sphere. Repeat on the other side.

step 3

5. Continue this pattern until you have used all large hole beads and spheres.

6. Place around neck and measure to desired length. Cut off any excess fabric.

7. Place each end of fabric in a crimp. Secure shut with jewelry pliers.

8. Twist open jump rings and attach one to each ring of each crimp.

9. Close one jump ring. Insert the lobster clasp into the other jump ring and close.

step 7

Read More

Hove, Carol. *Make It Yourself!: rom Junk to Jewelry*. Cool Makerspace. Minneapolis: Checkerboard Library, 2018.

Laughlin, Kara L. *Sparkle and Shine! Trendy Earrings, Necklaces, and Hair Accessories for All Occasions*. Accessorize Yourself. North Mankato, Minn.: Capstone Press, 2017.

Ware, Lesley. *How to Be a Fashion Designer*. New York: DK Publishing, 2018.

Internet Sites

Use FactHound to find Internet sites related to this book.

Visit *www.facthound.com*

Just type in 9781543525526 and go.